Damaged

A collection of poems

CRYSTAL WELLS

atmosphere press

This collection of poetry is inspired by my Teenage Nightmare.

When I was fifteen my dad passed away,

I was depressed, bipolar, self-destructive

I was on a search for love and understanding.

I was born out of the tar of my old life.

This is the story of who I used to be.

No-one wants to talk of the dark in which we can be encaged,

but the best thing for you to do IS TALK ABOUT IT!!!!!

These pages
are filled with the blood
of my Demons

I alone slain

When I was forgotten

When I was afraid

Table of Contents

Friable

Monsters vs Fae

beautiful sting

Wonder-lust

Wandering alone

crystal was such a wild child

crazy

imaginative

naive

She believed in faery tale dreams

She whispered with the trees

always cared for dead things

As we all know

Nothing is as beautiful

as the world

through the eyes of a child

Crystal, lost her innocence young

she had no idea what was to come

Sad to say

she hid herself away

Angry at the world

for feeling so cold

<u>*Hey you*</u>

Living inside your head
Hey you
Singing to the dead
Hey you
I found the answers
When Nothing Else Matters
Hey you
Depressed on your phone
Hey you
Felling all alone
Hey you
I fucking love you

<u>**In this place**</u>

I stand in a deserted street,

      In a stranded town,

All roads are closed,

Empty buildings,

Echoing memories,

Haunting me like a melody

We used to roam the avenues

             Just you and me,

Like we made this dead world

Come to life,

Now

Nothing has felt more dead to me,
Then this place,

           All things grow and die,

But for a moment,

      We were alive,

<u>**Are you just like me?**</u>

Dying to be free

I focus on my madness

    such sadness

  The only thing I feel

       Wondering if my wounds will heal

Hopping the feeling would decay

    Be that as it may,

      Everything turns to grey,

            My thoughts in disarray

        How a heart could betray

         Leaving it this way

         Escape the sorrow that I feel

           Razor romance

         What have I done

        to be judged by everyone,

Can anybody hear

   silent screams,

Bursting inside,

        Are you just like me,

         Dying to be free?

<u>All the wrong I've done</u>

and all the sad songs I've sung

for all the dead who still speak

for all the living who won't see

for all the pain I betray

for all the lies you let play

yes, darling, it's that time

I've let all things slide

> you're my beggar's rights

Giving up my life

I wanted her here with me

A mother's melody

My forgotten face

Family disgraced

By all the wrong I've done

And all the times they won

You could have never known me

Believe me this time

You're never on my mind

<u>**the art of letting go of you**</u>

so, we left things unsaid
      broken left inside a jar
             I never kept closed,
    pain seeps through me,
      like a disease
Coming to take me away,
He never listened when I'd say
I can't keep living this way
Never knowing how he feels
    I wish that love could be like it is in my dreams,
Sad to say
    Dreams are not reality
          There is nothing in fantasy he feels
the pain helps me heal, perspective what is real,
    Helped me keep focus
On what I truly
    needed to do,
    the tragic art of
      letting go of you
          you never understood my soul
        my spark my fire
      always trying some way to bring me back to the ground
        when I'd clime to high
        but darling when I fall
        it won't be for you

and they say it will get better

I scoff

Will it ever

They care so little for we

Whom feel forgotten and damned

We the unplanned

The promise

Led astray

I always felt so afraid

In a flash, it all changed

You couldn't see me

Stricken slain

Get better

Will it ever

<u>**Drifting into loneliness**</u>

Wondering in emptiness,

Can't shake this feeling

That I am in,

Like bugs crawling in my skin,

Blood drips down white walls

For you, my heart calls,

scars start to unfold,

be bold

the right words are lost within,

knowing I am going to hurt again,

 I wanted more than this

Endless ache

Reminded of every mistake

Things never turned out well

When no one thinks your special

Your Words

yelling at me

repeating

I mean not a damn thing,

Telling me "YOU'RE nothing,"

Creating a river inside

 to die

slowly rotting away

Never knowing

I am one of a kind

Made of real heart

faery soul

You love to tear me down

      place this pitiful frown

drowned by thoughts of suicide

          You are hurting me

 scaring mind Yelling

"YOUR'E NOTHING!!"

I always turn away

never listen to what I'm saying

What is the point of staying

the victim your portraying

you're a fucking grown man

act like it…

never born to win
tested
lost it all
stayed strong
it's a messy heart
doomed from the start
everything you water dies
poisoned inside

<u>**lost Thoughts**</u>

in a forgotten dream

cracks by the stream

Wanting someone to hold me tight

Wanting Something

that felt right,

when all went wrong

I lost my heart to a song

Keep on fighting strong

I know you've needed this so long

You lead me to the door

It wasn't blocked anymore

And lovely we learned how to fly

Lost thoughts

Take their time

Everything happens in the right mind
I found my home inside

I followed my own light

I changed my life

<u>Ragdoll</u>

I must be

you yell,   you scream,

You are always talking at me,

I am made of vain fantasy,

that You dream,

Sow my mouth shut

shall I never speak,

Cut out this

Fallen Heart,

It was worthless from the start,

DAMAGED

broken apart,

please blame it all on me,

I was not who you wanted to see

Bereavement and agony

Ragdoll dreams

And sad nightmares

Something here I'm not getting,

all though I cry

You keep forgetting,

Memory is made to pass,

my soul is made of glass,

Crystalized ash

I am just another deadhead,

Misfit gingerbread,

A porcelain face,

    missing affection

        crying for mother's attention

        Ragdoll she calls me

    All that you dream

          make me to be

                your doll

          your fantasy.

Nothing
you could ever do

Nothing

you could ever say,

Nothing

really matters anyway

in the dark

where shadows dwell

Nothing feels special

happiness

is ripped from the world,

and It felt so cold

knowing it was just nothing to you

when it was everything,

I could see

Forgotten

under that willow tree

Lonely love left to die,

for you and I,

we fucked it up this time

drowned in doubt

poison spills out

Only hopeless words

we sway

beloved cast astray,

No affection for you and me,

You killed what once shined within "we"

Deception and

treachery

You turn gold to stone

Killing everything you own

Trapped
      thoughts of dismay,

    death decay,

P
 U
  L
   L
    E   D
    D   O
        W
         N

To the underground

  Never thought a glow

    could grow so low,

  Lost in clouds of doubt,

always ripping my heart out,

  hiding pain within

Stuck stagnated

  same old sickly skin

      I bleed in

    another wasted day

Rotting my soul away,

      Worries

    Sorrows

      dreading tomorrow,

Is this pain home,

    The only one I have ever known.

Darling, now I dance with the dead

    The soundtrack of our end

And lovely it came to be

        No one is waiting out here for me

        Trapped

        in the shape of truth

            no one's looking out for you

<u>My soul is sinking,</u>

Is it's stupid thinking…

It's wrong to feel the way I do,

Always being blue,

Wanting something

I never knew,

Nothing ever came through,

alone fading away

Guilty for my pain

Waiting for the train,

pressure is to the skin

emptiness is seeping in,

nothing I have the will to do,

With all the pain

Death put me through,

Still

I move through the silence,

leaving behind senseless violence,

Giving my final goodbye

Taking my pathetic life.

<u>**Depression is the killer**</u>

When they love like a game,

it drives you insane,

pushing pulling

leaving your heart slain

This thing called love

eats you up inside,

taking over your mind

and you think

it will change this time

in the end,

Depression is the "sin"

you keep "giving in,"

It makes you sad

makes you lonely

like you're the only

person you'll ever have,

Tears seem to fall

Endlessly,

Depression is your enemy,

bring the razor

bring the pain

depression wins again,

thoughts of suicide

can't run or hide

the monster always finds a way inside

fighting back

the will of the heart

you couldn't from the start

Depression my killer

the only friend

when everyone leaves

the cycle starts again

Hunger

the whisper feeds

within

A staggering heart bleeds

Depression the killer

suffocating my flame

only the shadow shall remain

I think I lost myself again

<u>**I am only Hurting myself**</u>

Every day reminded of the same pain

cotton candy cocaine

reality hits me,

can't heal

racing conscious mind

escape an echo in time

start anew

if only we knew

how to feel another way

heal a heart, of lonely pain

Tend to every scar

the Remanence of where you are

she watched as I threw it all away,

never know what to say

it just won't be,

A faery can no longer fly

to get high

leaving me behind.

so lovely

I deconstruct every hurt

Was I ever good enough?

I hurt myself today,

Cutting the goddess out of me

beggars' blade
they called me insane

I felt like a sin

Such guilt I hide within

For being such

a disaster masterpiece

Bleeding all over the place

<u>**Something's**</u>

are simply not meant to be,

something is wrong with me

        is this how it all ends

   Still,

       with everything I've left behind,

          I've loved you for all of my life

          Beyond the veil of mind

          I've felt you all this time

          Why must it be

          You show no love for me

          Empty words

          Come what may

          I humbled my heart alone

          When you were nowhere to behold

          When you left me in the cold

I knew somethings aren't born to last

Somethings come and

       Something's

         pass

<u>Remember</u>

every tear

lost what I held dear,

many would come to say

they won't let love go astray,

Be that as it may

Everything turns to grey

Depressed in every way,

Pushed astray

some say,

it's not real

The Deep Sorrow we feel

Take this pain, beyond my years

Take these tears, that left the stain

Take this soul; glittering old

I am no longer here.

Defecated by ignorance

<u>Missing you became a way of life</u>

I wish on every star
      To be where you are,
      I want you to come home,
            Come back
                  to my brother, sister, and me,
                    Come back
                        to this insanity,

your little girl
      missing you, to the point
            she lost her self

How we couldn't see
      emotional turmoil in your eyes,
          sadness
             dripping from your soul
                    spreading to me
                      like a disease
You and I
      alone lost every night,
             committed to being misunderstood

Now I have nothing
      Left
            hallow and alone,
               a heart collecting stones,

I am as cold as
      one already dead,
            I died the same night you did

When I needed you,
          always there when I call

I should have known something was wrong

                    last time I looked in your
              sad hazel eyes
              you were crying
      you actually told me
          that you loved me

and
 I never saw you alive again

I couldn't see through lines
        I hear in my mind
                your final goodbyes,
                        how could I have known,
            where the lonely room,
                I would lose my home,

Life cannot be worth the pain,

 I dream to be
Where you are

Marshmallow sky
Among the stars

What are the Gods to gain
            puzzle pieces to a sick game

                        Daddies little girl
                            mad at the world
                            for losing its hope
                            and handing me the rope

<u>**No one remembers her face**</u>

lost in a distant haze,

a constant maze,

Suddenly,

the urge rises,

Wanting to rip off their disguises,

She doesn't need your false praise,

She's been wandering for days,

Sparkling soul began to fade,

trapped in razor blade romances

to sickened skin,

Such a sad girl,

sits alone,

nowhere to call home,

she roams

from place to place

No one remembers her face.

<u>Can it be real</u>

I don't know what to feel,
Deep
Down
I am just a sad girl,
screaming at the world
they never heard a sound

My soul is singing
heart keeps screaming,
Love me
I will never stray
I am left in dismay
everyone pushes me away
…I stand too close
Depression holds its sway
lost in seas of grey,
What would you say,
To this sad girl
Drawing stars in the sand,
When you know the sea tides,
to wash
little dreams away
would you show her your scars
tell her how far off she is from those stars
or would you let her believe
beauty is in everything

the haunting of fathers' past
this feeling forever lasts
there is nothing I'm letting go
It hurts me like a hole
agony and strain
I go through, losing the memory of you,
the sound of your voice
I couldn't call anymore
What hurts most
Is the feeling of your ghost
Reaching out to me

the day you died,
the world lost its light

just to see you again,
the stars I would reprimand
You gave me a taste of the end
A part of me will never mend,
You gave me,
All there is to give of death,
I have lost all of myself,
Stuck in suicidal thoughts, you planted
We took everything for granted
I wait under blanket clouds every night,
pray everything is alright,
I always cry myself to sleep
Is this why I've always loved such wicked hearts
Mommy and Daddy didn't love me from the start
I will always feel the same,

the fool to blame,
I couldn't see,
That you and I;
are one of a kind,
nothing alike
thought the truth of it all is,
I felt haunted in such a way
all you would say,
"loneliness holds its sway,
meant to live this way
don't even try to change
Condemned to dismay
none of you loved me anyway"
you pushed everyone away

a jolt to my senses,
when you would look at me,
with discontent in your eyes
Tell me "go play on the freeway",
You broke my heart
Like you never saw me
I wasn't a good daughter

How could this be

Memories flooding through me

My eyes fill with tears

suffering through all of these years

You are every tear I cry

Alone

I feel like someone else tonight

with the pits of my despair

You can't wash the pain away

Pretend it has been

forgotten with yesterday

A part of you still lives inside my mind

Floating in memories of time

<u>I have left behind me</u>

nothing

but

a Cruel Nightmare

I once had made mine,

a special passage of time,

I am trapped in this endless surrender,

my heart   "too tender"

it's all I have to
give

Maybe

I am defective,

becoming so defensive,

lost, stranded

in a foreign land,

Yearning for the touch of your
hand,

Leaving nothing

but ink stain,

Frozen in the snow

all I know is alone

Lost out in the cold

Growing tired, growing old,

Is my soul to be sold

Is there a point to being **bold**

I never know whom to call

when I know

I'm about to Fall

so, you'll never hear from me at all

Violent Heart-Storm

I want to change

to feel Warm

                    I live in a blizzard mirrored

with different killers,

      my heart constantly withers

There is always a chill in the air

    I wish I would disappear

    I don't want to die

                 All alone,

          I need to transform
       Embrace my heart storm

wishing for summer snow
sadness that we all know,
wonder what is wrong with me,
can't I be happy,
wanted a love,
a tender touch,
wanted it too much,
blind to see
It's not meant to be,
red flags don't mean help fix me
I just wanted to find my fish
In this endless sea,
I just want what is meant to be,
is that always the case
Running after something,
we cannot chase,
I feel like I am miles away from here,
can I mean something before I die
I just want what I cannot find,
I don't want to be a lost cause,
I wish I could put life on pause,
And heal the part of me
No one wants to touch

<u>Pretend</u>

with me,

like you understand

Taste the pain,

Count your sorrows as keepsakes

Kill happiness with internal turmoil

Broken spiral coil

know

I have always dreamed of death,

feeling alone inside,

wanting to die,

so maybe I could see my father again

maybe in another life

we can be together

as a family

<u>none can hear her woe</u>

not God
Soldier or soul
She is lost
full of sorrow,
where can she go,
Her immense heartache
full of remorse,
She fell of course
fumbling through tears of blood

forgiving a sin

tripping over love,

falling from above,

blood turned to ash
weeping from emerald eyes,

Burning holes in the skies

falling from grace

<u>**Where do I go**</u>

taken from my home

this pain,

destroying my brain,

It's driving me insane,

How do I reclaim myself again?

you may think it lame,

But

you've never watched the world fall

from shattered eyes

all walls crumbled down

claimed by the underground

Cataclysmic coffin hole

Destroyed everything

I dared to hold

And I had never

felt so alone

<u>**I didn't know What I do now**</u>

everything changed

the fool inside of me always looking for an escape

my head on the ground,

there is no one around,

I take the to the skin

Let out the pain within

my oldest friend,

Always been there for me in the end,

I know you never wanted it this way,

what else could I convey

I can't keep living this way

nor love a life

without you,

I am living pain,

spilling out goodbyes

drunk on sorrow

ghost calling home,

my suicide surprises

another fey lost their life

no one ever believed in me

they clapped for my replacement

<u>I play memories in my head,</u>

of you and me,

How things used to be,

when the sky starts to fall,

will you be there when I call,

my pillow shall embrace

every tear falling from my face,

the world you wanted me to see,

Now is

blinded from me

For all eternity

Into darkness, we fall

blinding agony,

mortification alchemy

the trauma makes us sick,

at our scabs we always pick,

endless Dread

constant Concern

Tending Mending

the lights that shine

an makes us whole,

in time we come to find

everything's dimmed and faded away

nothing sparkling this way,

desolation; left for you to see

hurting is but a dream,

the darkness calls us out to play,

Self-destruction on display

Only we who crave the end

Disappear into gloomy days

<u>mystified so close to home</u>

A world that claimed me for its own,

    things become

        so, messed up

            like running with no end

                twisting things

                    so slowly

you made me believe

    you were the one and only,

then comes a day,

    it's too tight to breathe,

the day the world suffocated me

 lies are crushing dreams

        nothing is what it seems

            ripped through the seams,

                Smashing my self-esteem

Wishing I could fix things

            No, not this time,

                Feeling is not a crime

Missing what was once mine,

            that place that felt like home

              a family I called my own

<u>**As I look back at it**</u>

I understand so much I couldn't put together
I was like a creature licking my wounds
I thought that if the death of my father enveloped me
I would finally be granted death
peace
But now I see
He lives beside me
I feel him when I daydream
Haunted by his smell
my guardian on the other side
I am a firm believer in your soul
whom you are you have always been
You're born of the earth and so with the earth
You shall remain
But my father
he stayed to guide me
a melody in my heart
connection firm still
a jar of dirt from his stone
On a mantel that I own
`his light keeps my darkness still
I've always loved my daddy
And I always will
Some ghosts heal the pain
Guiding the broken
Forced to stay

Friable

-    Easily crumbled to dust

I lost my marbles

in tea set tables

Dressed in black lace

Alice

in Damaged Wonderland

Eat me

Drink me

Kill me

It's all the same

This way

That way

Fuck this place

<u>**darkness throughout the land**</u>

Seeping creeping

Spreading like a disease,

We all beg and cry for a cure,

"can't take this anymore",

this is something

you would never ask for,

a disease of the mind

bipolar past time

all that we witness

all that we identified

is nothing but a lie,

Pretending that it is all right,

Seeing shadows

Through the light

Ghosts of another life

Look right through me

 I just needed her to see

the pain that creates me

holding it in every day

scared to say

My thoughts in disarray,

The sorrow and dismay,

Throughout the pain of these years,

Dripping with tears,

Crippling the dream

that flies so high

Inside that midnight sky,

aspirations seem
to die,

As love fades

Leaving the scars that remain,

Bleeding for love

I'll never understand

living like a stain

blood dripping

from a glass heart

her empty blue eyes

still look right through me

<u>All by myself</u>

lost on the inside,

no one to confide,

hide myself away,

I have nowhere to stay,

Don't you know,

I've let myself go,

motherfuckers never know

the pain began to grow

stuck on the inside,

I grow so low,

Withered away,

thinking like this every day

I just end up,

Letting depression win

the sadness in,

all by myself

I know that I will always be stuck in mclancholily

solemn,

lonely,

The last doll on the shelf,

Destined to be

All by myself

"she's too sensitive"

               still estranged,

      my heart

         dead drop,

         I just want it all to stop,

Wanting nothing more,

    to be the faery who would soar

         to be loved

          at my very core,

To be the one   a family did adore,

        I stand here the family whore,

      Never asking anything more

           Living in another world

           "She's too sensitive"

           Who asked you anyway

Do they ever think

Well I can be too critical

And cruel

Or do these people really think

They are above it all.

        Yes, I cry when you yell

      I flee when you scream

       I retreat for survival needs

You make me feel hated

Berated The loser bread

Never cared to see my suffering

<u>The forgotten faery</u>

harbinger of sorrow

decayed

felt betrayed

she never felt ashamed

to wear her jacket well

thorns chains

graveyard remains

loving lost souls

holding their space

why couldn't you see her

out of place

another brownie baby

goblin crazy,

the one with the spark

holding it all apart

the forgotten faery

spare

Just a Moment of your time,

Help ME

get back

what once was mine,

a sense of self

lost in time

give me

one last glance

For one more chance,

To Finally Fly

I Hear you

calling out my name,
 cutting out the pain,
"I never know what to say"
 it always comes out the same
always the misunderstood
ready to understand
all you needed
is a listening comrade
a friend so hard to find
everyone wants something
use me up and I'm done with you
I heard every word
        weren't you listening
little birdy left to die
pushed from home life

<u>*personality disorder*</u>

Nowhere else to go
no place to call home,
I can't hold on,
nowhere for me   *to belong.*
Screaming into the wind
In a silent corner of my mind
She whispers
"Hold on Darling
You've got to let it all Go
Keep Moving On

Follow your sad song.
and when
there is nowhere else
For you to go,
far from home,
Don't despair,
will be there your never alone
Don't bring yourself down"
I come in singing
can you save me
salvation
heart cries for creation
my mind
believes its lies

put it back
pull me back
bright side
I think the sun will shine
again
All the past is left behind   again
Our heart has no need to pretend,
a conversation with no end.
Maybe you're right,
I am always wrong.
no need to string me along,
Nothing is undone in a song
How could our mind mend,
when it's fighting with its self again?

<u>**Dizzy within a dream,**</u>

nothing, *I will say*
                    I drive them all away,
                        misery heartache
            homesick
            grief-stricken
                        and slain
            I squandered my needs again

I can't help think in such a way
            this demon inside my soul
                        Letting it take control,

I imagined that I could make it through
Screaming sad songs to the wind

                        Where will this crossroad bend

            is there a sequence to this trend

                        the loneliness blessed to end

                        things we didn't comprehend

            Where will your life turn

When all your faith is burned,

            For love was never returned,

Yet your soul constantly yearned,

            They always called you Damaged,

Thru the Sadness, you managed

                        thru every setback,

                        every disadvantage,

You concur, the most daring challenge,

            Even when every step

            you take in faith betrays you

                        I shall love you

heal your wounds,
Your bounds with no end,
Every broken heart you mend,
Every tear you tend,
All the sad letters you never send,

I'll hold you if you need to cry
We are all human inside
Dizzy within a dream
Poisoned mind
Household lines
Walk the tides
It's safe to say
You're led astray
They never knew
The power of a dream
The sacrifice in creating reality

<u>**Never feeling good enough**</u>

Born of human sludge
    going for the wrong hand,
       Damage a Wreckage
in supply and demand,
Why
  nothing goes as planned,
Nothing is just right
    Always crying
  lonesome poem nights,
     tired of trying to be
    bondage free

        Picking the wrong key
     begging   a plea
      pain, all to a halt
       such a degree
        beg for unity
      can you hear me
       to be me

All though
   I don't know who I am

       ......anymore,

  The person I thought I was to be

  has faded inside me

  they said she wasn't enough
   as I watched her slip away

<u>**all is Lost**</u>

        in the shadow of my mind

Love has failed

Left a hole Nothing can fill,

A pain, you graciously gave me

        "I am crazy"

You can't love the lost girls

When you're scared of the dark

      you don't know who you are

Can't sleep

      thoughts, awaken me,

Taunting me in my dreams

     Am I the lost soul?

     Too far out to find

     too blind to see

        howling alone I feel,

         I continue on

            my own

         Never revealing the hurt I feel

Never knowing the real me

      just

        The doll she dressed me to be

<u>**The saddest story**</u>

Ever told
happens to be true,
  Do you, even know you?
I'm desperate I cry out
bloody cutter, you'll never need another
 every heart you smother
  everyone gives up on you
 it stings the stitches you've sown
  always fighting on your own
I know the feeling
 Slowly dying
  rotting away,
You believe
this feeling will always remain,
All you are
  is broken hearts
   simple doll parts,
I know the smell
 blood so sweet
  Always putting up a fight,
   Love, never worked out right,
Feeling so misunderstood,
  Just like I would
   I have made it through,
    And so,
     can you.

<u>**Criticize me**</u>

Throw your shade
leave your blade
skipping rocks
over crystal towers
do you not see
the blessings that have lade me
while you poison yourself
                        your seed
with your wicked words
            leaching light
                    suffocating life

The sting of being misunderstood

<u>**My world is littered with shadows,**</u>

I await the gallows,

my heart lies in shards,

tattered game of cards

Could you promise me, one thing?

your love won't sting,

you'll listen while I sing,

I could give you anything,

I could give you my beating heart,

Toxic art

Been betrayed

darkness is all around,

New demons are being found,

I'm six feet in the ground,

But I can hear this sound,

A lover's melody, haunting

Like August Rhapsody,

It could cast the shadows away,

Make light of this grey,

And give birth to a new day,

I don't know how to live that way,

Life is killing me,

As you can see,

I am lost in misery,

someday,

I'll be alright, *no thanks to you*

fight for my right

to be the light,

I will embrace the night,

And shine

Like stars do

    forever bright,

How I've longed to be,

I'll be the mother of shadows

    I'll be the huntress

        the hallowed

  I'll be the guide

      The eternal night

        The forever sprite

    Dancing in the dark

I am that spark

    Casting shadows

That dance and sway

    Born to die

      Living to survive

Learning

  how to thrive

You can hate me

But I look at it this way
> I loved him more than you
>> You called me a killer
>>> I'll never be a winner

You're so much smarter
> I'm just a sinner
>> I spent years
>>> Wanting your affection
>>>> You always denied me

And that's okay
> I learned on my own
> *Don't crawl back*
asking why
I'll never fight for you again

Falls Apart

From the start
I thought I was going to lose

nothing more than a broken heart,

nothing more than falling apart,

I keep looking for the strength

to reflect on open eyes

understand Damaged lines

what I was losing out of life.

Sometimes, it takes so long for me to see,

Nothing is how it should be.

I beg to be free.

Sometimes, love goes wrong,

Sometimes, you are not strong

you can't move along,

forgot your Favorite song,

Sometimes

My world will crash,

my insides all turn to ash,

Burning darkness over day,

Nothing was ever the same,

How do you forget a name?

how do you forget a heart?

how do you, repair?

When everything,

Falls apart.

The Mask

in which I hide
must protect the person inside

The sweetness

I will never reveal

For the bitterness keeps it still

Behind the grim mask

love unseen

Behind undiscovered

I am free

No one can hurt me

death masks reflecting the empty

Allows feelings to hide

Never showing

the inside

The damage

That you can't see

Protecting this person inside me

So, you know

not to Fuck with me

freedom I have never felt

a dream never dreamt

How much, your actions affect me

The mask in which I hide

locked away

to never find

This person

You will never see

For you will never let me

just be me

I've got to defend myself

from your narcissistic personality

<u>**In a world where everything hurts,**</u>

Nothing is ever going to feel the same,

There is something wrong with my brain,

Pain making me insane,

      every touch kills

  I'd rather be eating dirt,

Every muscle aches it hurts

      – how much can a body take?

  bed my new best friend,

      don't worry we'll be together again.

I used to love the rain,

      sweet sound cleaning the air

            the crisp smell of her hair,

What I wouldn't give to go back when

        Touching didn't hurt my skin

      feeling every Pressure within,

I used to wake up early in the morning refreshed,

Now head gets dizzy memory is frizzy,

It's a hassle to just get dressed,

      with this weight on breast

every day I try my best,

never getting very far,

Feeling every scar

can't take this constant ache,

a battle within

feeling sinking in,

my head starts to spin,

I pray to the Gods

I wish to die, disappear

I took advantage of my life

What else is to remain

In a world, of advancing pain

Shall this be

The end of me

Chronic decay

Growing empty

<u>**Depression is only in our minds**</u>

but it's killing me all the time.
They proclaimed they never knew why
Endlessly I cry,
Lose my mind,
I forgot my heart this time,
Not knowing
Why I stay,
When I should go,
to die in every way
Nothingness
Decay,
No reason to go on,
Please remember me
I don't understand,
Who I am

I don't want to give up
This pain inside
I don't want to forget what it was like
the day he died

Stuck in this frame of mind,
couldn't hold back,
All turned to black
through the cracks of broken skin

I was a scab within

to die in every nightmare

agony surge through me

as Nothingness melts away

Losing myself in decay

I can't fly

When I am Dead Inside,

I Want to believe the lie he gave

Someday it will all change

Depression is only in our minds

yet mine

is eating me alive,

I see every flaw

Love claimed to not see

A reflection of empty.

<u>So much you can't see</u>

I forgot myself

Nightmare it had to be

 For good dreams aren't born of truth

Lovers lost it came to me

I forgot the weight of your fantasy

The hell of this leaving

To the other side

So, you couldn't see

Darkness stripping me

Eating my fleshy soul

When I died alone

I barely made it back

       from the underground

and when I came too

there was only you

<u>lost</u>

solemn lonely

no way I can do this on my own,

is there an easier way

where I don't have to live this way,

sit in therapy all day

I don't want to face the stain

this sorrow

twisting inside of me

turning into someone

I didn't want to be,

I thought it would be easy

to fall

wanting to cut too deep,

the Pressure sinks in,

through the cracks of *my Broken skin.*

cut out this defeat,

I am the Loneliness.

these tears

these scars

being young is so painful

<u>**He was my Dad**</u>

even when

running away words cursed by tears

always glancing back,

for anyone dare to Fallow,

always felt so hollow

yes, for years we watched,

As daddy would walk out the door

Saying the same thing as before,

too young to understand,

I just did not want daddy to be sad,

I would try little things to let him see,

How wonderful he was to me,

never made a difference

It was not until I had realized

shaking staggering a voice,

I learned I had a choice,

not sit back,

As all did before,

Watch as daddy ran out the door,

gunslinger man

Uttering the same words as before,

"you're not wanted here, you wish I'd just disappear, you never loved me."

I used my voice to shake his hand,

Showed him that it is not all so bad,

What a beautiful family we had

I was glad he was my Dad.

<u>All my life,</u>

I've been locked up inside,

Destroying my own frame of mind,

I tell myself that

Inside my heart,

All broken DAMAGED torn apart,

robbed blind,

As if I am not part of mankind,

This soul is so full of sorrow,

Praying for a better tomorrow,

I wish I could be,

better for you,

better for me,

No matter how hard I try,

I can't keep that belief in my mind,

That I am one of a kind,

I just can't believe in me,

It's just how I was made to see,

all the worthlessness inside of me,

In my face, I see no beauty

my heart I feel no value,

my soul feels wild,

Unclaimed and free,

Like a supernova

Is growing inside of me,

I just want to shine, Like never before,

When life is not a bore

I want this and nothing more,

Therefore,

    it has come to see,

I am dead like dreams,
When you cling to me,

      I shall leave,

    I am made of these broken things,

My heart,

Is an endless winter,

    Weathering storm

    Wolf born

      so much inside of me

        I couldn't comprehend

          Sleeping with the dead

        Born of star shipped dreams

         Keeper of light

          blessed keys

Mending all who cross

    While they barely remember me

I would gladly give my life away,

    I wouldn't stand in your way,

        I want what is best

            for everyone else,

  With little care for myself,

    I will help you

    give it my all

        whenever I can,

           It's just who I am

<u>What were we doing</u>

Pretending
it would last this time,
looking
for what I will never find,
let it fool me
Down through the shattered glass,
our crystal hearts
caught in this crashing hour
soul
the will
the demon devours,
I need a hero
save me
from gravities spiral,
an everlasting emptiness,
What was I thinking
pull me down,
He took all that I ever had
threw it on the open ground,
Leaving me
alone with death
His kiss
kept my last breath,
could he know
what he had done
cried out to everyone
Could it be
we never cared for me
What were we doing
love we were pursuing,
darkness we came to be,
all the light of life left me.

<u>**fight to be free**</u>

from darkness

dwelling

swelling

compelling

my sparkling

dark soul

Triggering

thoughts in my mind

Deadlier

then any poison,

violent thoughts

controlling my will,

No need to break free,

I'm far too broken

From words unspoken

I keep them all locked here

I'll always have some reason to feed what they say

to feel,

not good enough

Mental torture

suffocated my soul,
I never felt whole,
Something went missing,
I don't know how to find,
I believe it's my state of mind,
Always coming back
to a past so black,
pain born of me
made to see,
darkness inside of me,
what we've become
at the end of a hopeless man's gun
loneliness for all too see
but still, no one understands me
Those whom I love most,
as deaf as a post,
could you taste every drop of blood sung
listen as they sway
milling on
trying to understand,
sadness gets in the way
it keeps me
still here

So hard
moving on
wandering daughter
tired
find the light
darkness is your life

Somehow it has become home
how to be happy all alone
how to feel right,
find the light
It is hard to know if someone really cares
No one is ever there
my happiness is no one's responsibility

I'm sorry for being a bother

Cold and Bitter

I didn't know any better
                lost alone
          how do we see
     when all is lost from me
how do we feel
     when everything was never real

          everything has gone numb

                    how could I have been so dumb?
                         meant this to be
                              forever
                         and after

          is there a life out there for me to find?
               the real me locked inside
     Trapped
          in my broken mind,
The trauma response
          My soul is lost,
          My heart damaged by your hate,
               It's made me feel so cold
                         so bitter,
               Frozen, in endless winter,
          Should I set myself free?
And lead a life that I want for me,
Sparking like the forest frost
          There is much I would love to see
               A life of Adventure awaits me.
I don't have to be cold and bitter
     I can heal myself
          for me

<u>**dying inside**</u>

can't get it off my mind
                Love
        has never really
    felt kind

Everyone throwing that word around
Like they know what it means

        They don't know a Fucking thing
The love so selfishly
        Ignoring your

        Regrettably

                what we had couldn't be called love,

place the cuts on my skin
Self-destructive ecstasy
my pain escapes free
through the trails of blood
                        Everyone hates me
                                When I hate myself

                        I can be stronger than this
                I'll learn to stand
                                        on my own two feet,
My revenge will be sweet

Fight for Your Life

For the sight,

To see your-self again

Can't let the loneliness win,

Listen to the song

of everything,

No matter what pain you may endure,

you can take
more,

the faery of dark despair,

will be there,

guiding you through your darkest
hour,

Your pain she will devour,

And a ray of hope,

shall shine in diamond eyes,

shaking in your soul to a
standstill,

and again

you will

fly high

flourish in the blue sky

No longer

will you speak of goodbyes

You have the power

to win

the fight for your life

<u>mending all the tears</u>

your memory ripped in my heart,

living in agony

      All the words that tore me apart,

all the shards of my broken heart,

      left me to blind to see,

         How beautiful I came to be

I belong somewhere I feel free.

   True identity

  Mask be free

         Feel the sun

On my forgotten face

Healing feels like bleeding

In toxic waste

<u>**Narcissistic man**</u>

no, I'll never understand

I'm just trying to be

a better me

Forgiving those last
fights,

Following the bright lights,

moving on from past lives

I never have to feed you again

Monsters vs Fae

<u>It feels like a piece of me is missing,</u>

It hurts like a piercing

stinging sorrow

Because tomorrow,

never comes,

And for forever,

I have been searching,

Fighting a war inside

Heaven Vs Hell

I knew it to be

An angel couldn't save me,

This demon takes me away,

With all this sorrow and sway,

Everything turns to grey,

could never shine a light,

That would burn forever bright,

To shine upon me,

set my soul free,

I just want something,

No one could ever give me,

I want what could never be,

A change of destiny

<u>**darkness is holding me still,**</u>

I feel I don't have the will,

my body has gone ill

how do I fix it
I say

when all I have ever known to be

led me astray,

Just tell me what to do

I'd gladly suffer for you

To be free from the monster inside of me

<u>*Today, in Therapy*</u>

The so-called Dr. Scott

Took the devil's
Side

And I cut myself
With my mirror knife
In the bathroom
Down the hall

Why does the devil always win

It's like they can't see

He's a monster within

Playing in Angels skin

<u>**My Twisted Reality**</u>

Every day I crucify myself
        the living damned,
                no matter what others may say,
     no cure, love could hold
 an endless battle I fight
To keep He the darkness at bay,
            It becomes so heavy
        I have lost my sanity,
There is no one to blame
     I let myself slip and fall,
           The struggle of it all,
    Step into my mind,
        The nightmare,
           I have come to believe,
             My twisted reality

I've got to be the hero this time

<u>Yes, it's true to me</u>

Shadow normality

I see her glancing by

Her whispers eat me alive

She is so mean to me

Saying exactly what he trained her to be

Mocking all my insecurities

Mirror mirror on the wall

Who's the dumbest of us all

The you You play for we

The same self you claim to be

Yes, its true to see

Shadow normality

You're the monster

You see

Reflecting mocking

Your living tragedy

<u>As Demons Do</u>

Dance in my sky
    an ache created beating inside

          I'm all alone now
    he remains in the ground
        Nothing worth living for,
Streaming guilt like ever before,
I can feel the bleeding
stabbing ache of breathing,
all the pain
from living,
If only I knew how
    to pull myself
      from this ditch in the dark,
        not let the demon rip me apart
    stop the bleeding in my heart,
This damp hole in which I lie
    coved in lye
      Consumed by pain
        caught in a rage
        loneliness I can't contain
          all the sorrow of loving you so.
My heart became this ditch
    A hole too big to Stich,
      Darkness I have never overcome
        only understandable by some.
Shall I ever lift my head from the ground
    this sorrow remains deep down
    will you look for me
      Shall you see
      Misery is what makes me

 I have been waiting
    To be free
From the pain
    I hold so dear
      If only you could taste this fear
      awaiting to die here
I feel so hallow
    when I am all alone
      looking for that place to call home

96

I never know what to do
                              love has left me so
                                        felling like never
                    before
              only to make your heart sore
        I am frightened by this fear,
                        yet I want to keep it near,
I am haunted by the dream

Demons dancing
        in the ash of sky,
        Angels' screaming a cry
                    Death comes
                            before dawn,
        the Darkest part of life
death has you in her sight,
Where will you run?
Where will you hide?
                    Now that you're
                        Damaged Inside.
            The Demons have come for you
with
        all the pain
                that you ever knew,
Pray that death is near,
there is only you,
Dying
As Demons Do

<h2 style="text-align:center"><u>This disease</u></h2>

Burning my world away,

his neglect came in seeding,

Growing this monster of decay,

that ate my soul away,

I was crumbling with regret,

And after all this time

I didn't know what I was thinking,

I didn't just walk away,

When monsters were causing
such decay,

now that you're gone,

days grow ever long,

never knew I could get so low,

I swear this time

I am done with you,

I curse the stars above, with your name

Millions of chances you've destroyed,

when I was sad

you were annoyed,

that's how I knew

you couldn't be the one

my world became lonesome,

heart began to freeze,

You came into my life sprouting this
disease,

No matter what I spray,

I can't wash you away

broken hearts we created,

Love never grew

just faded

All I've loved

became all I ever hated,

the most bitter of sweet loves I've tasted

You came upon me like a disease,

A sea of black debris,

No longer will souls sing,

This disease

killed everything

<u>Child of Lies</u>

you see

what does it mean to be in your reality

a faery you can't feel,

angels you don't see

reach for you

Calling out your name,

Do you love me

am I just pretend

While I wait for

Cataclysmic damage to mend

to be the end

I can feel the cracks in my heart

to live

to breathe

him here with me,

ever the fatherless child

I know now

the unwanted one

you deserve better,

A girl wouldn't cut or cry

always fighting to get high

obsessed to death

All you could want

a child of lies

 puts on a disguise

never tells you how they feel

someone that is not real,

You just don't get it

You don't understand

This disaster you created your plan

You couldn't see me

Or worse

You saw exactly what was happening

And you did nothing to protect your daughter

Left her for the slaughter

A child born to feel, the will of woe

You let her spark go

in the subtle heartbeats

failure is all you see

Not the real me

not who you wanted to be,

complacent with abuse

what's your excuse

Disregard my existence

the scared broken child

Someday you shall see

you led me to believe

All you hated

was me

never a perfect kid,

This isn't building a bitch

To pick and choose the will of a
heart

You can't help

who your kids grow to be

Cry out is all I did

broken family consequences

Dress a child of lies

Worn,

torn,

with a girly disguise.

<u>We waited so long</u>

forgotten moments turn to dust

waited so long in endless night,

Feasted on blood

red wine,

searching for my kind,

All of these demons are mine,

Soulless with an active mind,

an emptiness inside,

No words could ever write,

We take it in stride,

Reliving the day, we died,

loved ones cried

caught by the landslide,

Some had a guide,

To the afterlife,

Where I walked alone

a bumpy ride it was,

a life of decay and dust

No way of knowing trust,

We belong to no-one

Monsters of the midnight sun

Soulless

with an active mind,

Dead

still alive

<u>**With a sadness I thought,**</u>

do broken hearts really mend,

I feel every tatter

ever scar

the remanence

of your touch

we lost so much

all I see

is the bitter end,

Fractured, dissolved

Disorganized

Dark Thoughts

contorting my mind,

leaving me blind.

Memories consume

angel hearts

scars polish and feed

growing monsters inside

a fractured mind

soul too dark to see,

the Demon stirring inside of me,

<u>Darkness</u>

understands

the waves of my bereaved soul,

Darkness

all that has ever been,

Beating

brokenness

such torture

I cannot bear,

there is no time

we can't mend.

So,   they say,

I would never amount to a thing,

They kept tearing at my skin

Revealing the hurt

such sorrow within

I know it hurts to heal

Reliving the pain

We want to put behind

Another forgotten blocked-off nightmare

King of Sorrow

Master manipulator of tears

Hide my shadow

Throughout these years.

Forever, to cry at night,

Alone in bed,

Sorrow fills this room,

Slowly I start to die,

Watching you walk away

In disgrace

my face you did erase,

A poisoned heart

Left to fall apart,

King of sorrow

Burn me alive,

this fire consumes me,

My flesh starts to swell

heart begins to sing

and yell

The king of sorrow

killer of tomorrow,

I thought life had just begun,

shall no longer walk in the sun,

damned to this hell

Feeling sick and not well,

these flames eat me alive

that my strive, holy survive

Let hope die

not meant to fly

I fall

Sowing my flesh

seam by seam,

a loving home was just a dream

she never saw me

bleeding

The king of Sorrow,

Stands at the devils' side,

Whispering taunting teasing

how he ended a life,

selfish suicide

As they say,

They never asked if I was okay

I can't comfort

My own broken soul,

The king of sorrow,

Came to be,

The master of deaths facade

Set ablaze

my tortured soul.

I survive the ever storm
fragile like a bomb

Kevlar heart stone

In darkness I was born

Nothing can tear me apart.

I'll explode and take half the city with me

<u>**Feeling so low**</u>

I lost my glow,

Every day

moves so slow

I never know where to go.

I've lost my home

no longer wanted

no longer needed

nothing more than a shadow.

Lost in the past

I forgot my path

I wanted something that would last,

forever.

Something that didn't feel so empty

I'm just a placeholder

Thrown away

To be used again

Uncontested temporariness

<u>**I hate my mind**</u>

It makes me feel crazy,
been left to die,
life is worthless,
Nothing on the surface,
No one understands why I am still sad
No one cares to be there
Everyone runs and hides,
It's better than knowing
what's on my mind,
I hate everything I see
when I look back at me,
the scars I try to cover,
Holes left by a lost lover
I feel trapped inside a monster
bi-polar roller coaster
Such tragedy
Haunts my family,
Maybe happiness,
Is something you
Always have to fight for,

<u>**can't go back to yesterday,**</u>

things will never change

You're still a monster, in my mind

The demon in the dark

who broke my heart
tearing the world apart,
If only you could see
that wound created me

an eternal dream

falling apart

s......e......a....m...... by seam,

sure, I forgive you

while I forget you

<u>**A girl torn**</u>

waiting to be Reborn

Lost, always Alone in a crowded room

        what life is there to live

           when they see you

                as this "sin"

You don't listen to what I say

what the point in trying anyway

I am this girl

lost soul

out to sea

      I am this fear

      shaking inside of me,

              currently, the end is near,

          become that fear and fright

            taste despair gives them a scare

              I know the pain

          you see,

        That monster of me,

You don't know,

      terror makes me,

              You have become a mess of me,

          Rotting endlessly,

                  Separating me

                    from starlight

        Damming me into darkness, where

Sir. Shadows dwell,

My own personal hell

Now the monster is I

you cannot abide

Every life ends in time

there I will be,

Dying with

this monster inside of me

<u>All a Dream</u>

I thought I knew

this man

I gave my heart too

I can remember

A place we used to go

Reaching out to the stars

making out the shapes of hearts

we used to talk

when all that's left is white lines

in each other's eyes

it falls now

like another life

never saw through your lies

till it was too late

you've changed my fate

Master of my sorrow

King of no tomorrow

Was I

such a fool

falling in love with you

you Hurt me

again,

and again

and I let you

dead within

eternal strife

Hell is where we must stay

sorrow, and sway

Pain forever to remain

There is no tomorrow

Decaying a new way,

It hurt to real this time

I gave my heart away

Love as a lesson

Embroidered on cotton hearts

<u>**Some might say I am crazy**</u>

(she tends to be lazy)
It's a chronic illness you selfish Basterds
I just need
Someone special
you see
Chameleon Eyes
not all can find,
A soul That sings   with a rhyme,
always feeling left behind

yes I hide those feelings
for not all to see,
they could hurt me
and they often do

you sit sticky
and stew
watch,
monster of the mind
eat myself inside

<u>There is a thought</u>

deep within my rotting mind,

     I am in that same Box

      as I have always
      been,

I have tried everything

    and nothing,

  still
  I can't break free

from whatever it is holding me,

    let's make the pain go away

    Just for a day

   Nothing can keep the demon at bay
  Still holds its sway

  I tell myself

    it's meant to be that way,

    I am meant for this pain

    It's like a shot to the brain

    Losing my sense of self again

    Such guilt I carry
from being weak and weary

   Never allowing myself rest

   To make sense of this mess

what is it I have here
        meant to fade
            and disappear

you all will be thankful,
    everything is perfect and tranquil

                    when I am no longer here
                        Suffocating in fear,
I won't stay to be his punching bag
I refuse to play these games
Can't you see
You've bonded with a monster
Can't you feel
The tension suspension
Will he raise his hand

Now you see
I've got this innate ability
To cut you free
From the ties
That bind you to me

beautiful sting

<u>Nowhere to go</u>

no one loves you so,
I guess it's all for the best
to learn all the same,
they all fade away and disappear
if only I could learn
to love myself
as deeply
as I've loved
everyone else

<u>**spectacular**</u>

is it meant for me

Wandering heart wanted to sing
Shine
how my heart could swing,
all the happiness
lovely distractions could bring,

It doesn't mean anything at all,

a heart's will

always falling
catching stars

<u>**You have known me**</u>

Through everything,

      your sparrow that loves to sing,

         never wanted loves bitter sting,

My heart deceives me

    I give it away so freely

My head

    refuses to believe me,

Loving heart Created to suffer

      Trust me   I can tell

          anger

        is placed well,

      when everyone lets you down

    you don't need anyone around

heartbroken
Beating in silver chest,
 just won't give it a rest,
 heart swears he was the best,
 broken, Torn in two,
Keeping little from falling in love,
With anyone but "you"

Time rolls on
He has moved on,
still all alone,
Forgetting self-control
 nothing to do,
            except stare at longing past pictures OF YOU
 I am holding myself back,
heart bruised black and blue
        the very meaning of life has died,
 truth be told
                broken heart free from cold
 chests empty
        lost inside
        questioning life's
                never-ending test,
        Destiny knows best
        so sick of this,
Feeling like the end

<u>**And if it is**</u>

what you say,
Your feelings for me have gone away,

There is little room in your heart
for me to remain
I'll let you leave

Why would I want you to stay

Don't look at me like that

I can hear it now

Lovely looking for a vow

Oh, darling can't you see

He is only saying those things

Actions never meet his words

Little lies and spurs

Stuck in place of pain

Real Love

    doesn't feel that way

Looking for Romeo

the light, of all that is good,

faded away,

Into darkness,

everlasting night,

Poisoned by the obvious,

A consuming loneliness,

They didn't know me from the start

I had a good heart,

With the grace of an angel,

He came to save me,

when I didn't need a thing

My knight in shining armor,

Saving me from my stepfather,

Oh, how I love you so,

my Romeo,

Dangerous, Romantic, Tragic,

Your love is like magic,

Circumstances Simply meant to be

taking over me,

Juliet, you call to me,

meet under the big oak tree

"We have nights cloak,

To us hide from their eyes"

I can no longer live a life of lies,

Please tell me

there is a way, you are going to
take me away,

All love stories start out that way,

Your words come out so smooth,

I don't even know how to move,

Is this all in my head?

now my cousin is dead,

It's like a curse with no end

I am looking for Romeo again

<u>Words escape me</u>

I don't know what to say,

I just want to write it all away,

Find a new way to survive the day,

I do not need to feel this
way,

Words escape me,

I don't know who you want me to be

Darling, that is not me,

I am already free,

As wild as could be,

I thought, that's why you love me,

I am never afraid to be who I am,

Words escape me,

You don't understand what I say,

Should I say it anyway?

I think not,

That will never be,

You could never understand me,

I create my destiny,

The words escape me,

I dare not speak,

I write about you,

While you sleep,

Wondering,

What secrets do you keep?

Slowly

so slowly
       I become the light and the dark
In every way
     you mend and break
      my fair
          fair heart
               Why must you
            tear it all apart
That is how days end,
    Any time now
         you stop loving me
            stop needing me
         you evaporate from my life
to come waltzing back in the nick of time
 tricking me to believe
That I will always belong to you
And so foolishly I always forgive you
      I really need someone
         No care what poison I am to drink
     Just help me not think
         Speak the words
     The lie in mind
         I love you
I'll always be
    Loves faithful fool
    Watch me die for you

<u>**we sit under the stairs**</u>

shelves of

dust dreams

in jar hearts

cement the walls

you touched my leg and leaned in

whispering to me

"Love is pain when I look at you"

he pushed me down

Never thought
Fate had mastered

Now I see you are just a bastard,

Thinking I'd let you get away with it
my heart is black and gold
your soul dismissed
dead

It is the stink of evil
that you bring,
Decaying everything,

All the horror you place
in hearts of the living,
die,
dance,
and cry
Leaving alone
nothing inside

<u>**By my blood undone**</u>

You lied to everyone,

    Causing pain is your fun,

Every day you mend and break

        my tell-tale heart

    Always ripping my soul apart,

        It is a fine art,

          This game you love to play,

           All those things

              you used to say

         Just to make me stay,

      You never loved me anyway,

       my blood undone,

          I don't belong to anyone

<u>**Eyes closed**</u>

I am bittersweet love
I fall when you leave,

    leaving my soul to grieve,

    the death of everything

 the blood in my heart

    Is particularly tart,

        growing sour from the strain

      leaching the mystery games

          of love and pain,

    a sickness of the brain,

It becomes so hard to believe,

I bring about this misery,

    Destruction university

      Out here with endless scars

        I am spun out so far

    I forgot where you are,

Lost in the park,

    I am stuck in the dark,

    as my eyes Close forever.

<u>In the cold</u>

lost lonely growing old,
Love a fantasy,
Running toward something you can't see,
It's only me,
in a daze I can't break free,
lost in the trance of a song
And the beat goes on,
Watching the December snow
The low starts to grow
Wondering if I reach out to you,
Will you still push away?
Love
the forever Dream
wonderful like a lullaby
that crashes to the ground
Wondering if you're singing along,
To all my sad songs
You only see the version of me
You wanted to be
of shiny things, silver rings
never knowing
Pain the silence brings
Frozen in the snow
life has grown old,
all I feel is the bitter alone,
Lost out in the cold.

<u>your fire eyes</u>

reminded me

you only see a side of meat

when your gaze

beamed at me

my life flashed cardstock
memories

little girl feels left behind

silenced by a knife

broken promise lullaby

Could I ever again

Believe in you
with all you put me through,
so much that makes me
a fragile heart,
Broken, tattered, torn,
a heart, covered in thorns
waking dragons' sleep
if you can truly believe
in me

no man's land
a faery in desert sands
catching jasmine stars
thriving in the dark

<u>**I remember first kiss,**</u>

How a heart can swing and miss

asking

was it all one beautiful lie,

convincing alibi

Feeling damaged inside

Will you love little ole broken me

However, Damaged I may be

I need love Larger than life

To combat this sorrow

Ragging, dwelling inside

Shattered broken apart

a withered heart

Tell me could it be

Loving you

Is for

Fixing me

How selfish is that to be

Needing a Hero to save me

However, Damaged I may be

I could never let you suffocate me

Vindication reserved for first kiss

Trash

is never missed

<u>**Words can mend the world**</u>

Yet, mean nothing new.

Alternative view

Your eyes I see thru

Looking thru me

crystalized ash

born to pass

We all tend to drift away

putting an end to it every day.

I need you now forevermore

I need your love like summer snow

today is forgotten

helping hands

How could you stand by

Let it all die

set me on Fire

watch me Burn

how could you take a turn?

I still needed you
Needing me

I keep falling

every day disintegrated

Can you catch me

It's too late,

I come crashing to the floor,

nobody wants me anymore.

Does all truth

Come to light
   Or does a liar's heart
        Fear
A Liar's fate
     Hate
      What you
        Yourself
          Did create,
    Only in darkness
     You are awake,
         The lies
       a life did take,
    so many hearts
      it did forsake,
   Lies,
like an earthquake
    So many lives
      it did shake,
   You created
Your own mistake,

A liar's fate
  You do await.

<u>**murderer of everything**</u>

born of

Hell, and Hawthorn Hart

Bittersweet sorrow

compels me to demonstrate

all the webs you weave

Fuck you

and everything you said to me

Forget everything

We claimed to be

You're just lost

clenching at spoons

forgetting

your hurt inside.

Heroin apatite

I couldn't stay there

and watch you slowly kill yourself

<u>What good is love</u>

when you never look inside

    when it makes your heart cry.

        What good is love

    When all you see

                you despise,

What good is love

    we can't repair

        when nothing is there,

                when you ran

                and let it die

when you fill it with your lies.

What good is love

    when you've gone

    and stayed away,

    when you never know what to say

    so, you say:

        Nothing at all

What good is love

when your feelings you don't comprehend

when you can't lend a hand,

    when all you do is demand

what good is love

  when your soul you must defend,

    fighting with no end

What good is love

when there is no longer a dance,

   when there is no longer a chance,

What good is love

 when all you do is go,

   treating it like your foe?

What good is love

when you never take your time?

   Couldn't care for what was mine

What good is love

 when someone can't say

What good is love,

 when you treat it this way?

<u>**Could you find it in your heart**</u>

you once did,

To look at me,

dare to see,

look past the ache

of a heart pain

take this sorrow away

hold me in your arms,

deep within you see

You're the universe to me,

Look at me,

I can show you the sky,

Sparkling the story,

of you and I

go back to where it all began,

time flashing through

watering eyes,

When love is all we had

we had a fighting chance

to flourish

the way we are,

I only wanted

Till the end of time,

Now, you are no longer mine,

our love shall never be again,

When all is sad

and done,

I always think of
you in a song,

Are you unforgiven too,

for he who lost the key

to my hidden door

that fateful day,

a part of my heart died

<u>All the Same</u>

everything changed
flip of the switch
you burned that bridge
Looking for another person to blame?
Can't you, handle your own shame?
You caused it all the same,

It hurts to even speak your name.
Thinning of the harm you've done
You turned love into a nightmare

I lose my head,
Thinking of you
the spark
I once saw in your eyes,
soul consumed by lies,
broken down every night, a part of me dies
he was born to break my heart
I will never understand,
Just as you refuse to see,
how you needed me,
Is everything all the same
everyone I've loved is dead
dealing with endless pain,
I always believed,
Love was worth every sacrifice,
That we could find paradise,
You burn to the ground

And darling,
I know you're terrified
I know love may blind
and mystify
such heart I can't deny,
My soul will always yearn to fly
through everlasting night
lost sight,
may all be the same,
I will not live-in shame,

Someday, it will not hurt,
        To utter your name,
Someday,
        everything will change.

alone in a cold room
only loneliness may loom,

Every night
always the same,
Sadness leaching on my brain,
never knowing what's to gain,
Always searching for a new way
to keep the darkness at bay,

daylight dreaming
of a new light
shining bright,
bringing hope
cradled in sun-kissed hands

Will this keep the loneliness away?
not the way you wanted it to be,
the way I was conditioned to be,
see the good in bad people
everyone has the potential to change
that's my toxic trait

<u>Charmed Fey illustrated for you</u>

love can be true,

mystically she taught you to heal

your Achilles' heel

Fought with you

made it through
To fall as we all do

To dream   *like a fool,*

For all these things

and more,

For you, calling her a whore,   so much she's been dying to say,

you never Stay, always running away

These empty screams

haunt Damaged dreams,

What is the point of this

Devote it all

to watch them leave

they all say these fucked up things,

I feel so small

a bitter sting loving broken things

it knows no true devotion,

hearts grow cold

love games grow old

Replacing the problem

No one could solve em'

Where we so easily Forgotten

As love went rotten.

<u>**Shame**</u>

        calling my name, placing the blame

devolution of my brain

      reveal anima again

Such a shame

       suffocating dark flame

           needing love

               to overcome such strain

                    stop the signals in my blackened brain,

                   I lost myself again,

Shame   my name

            fighting fail   to no avail

feel the same

nowadays

    as stagnant as tomorrows

      could of, should of, go away

                            unfortunately, I remain

                watch me as I decay

                  stripped my soul away

the heart contains suffering

           there are no goodbyes *when everyone dies,*

     in our world of lies

        everyone wears a disguise

        vanishing before sunrise

   passions were inflamed

       when *Shame* came

          to claim my *name.*

What was Once to Gain

His inks left a stain
Crawling through the cracks of
broken skin
emptiness sinking in,
Words you should say
could take this away,
that constant reminder
if he wanted to
he would be
communication
is key
he never listened to me
heart struck and bleeding
barely breathing
stuck in the feeling
what was once to gain
when love didn't invite more pain

Shattered heart started to mend

wounds

buried deep in my skin

the demons keep trying to get in

tears I weep

If only love could keep

all her broken promises

if I could just, be

happy in my own company

others words lead me

Forgotten afraid

So far astray,

power of light

Flow into my life

Letting it keep me alive

A power I cannot devise

My shattered heart started to mend

I felt like me again

She saw the stars in my eyes

She believed I would fly

Revolution to be free

I am not, what your words make me!

<u>**run from me**</u>

you fear
Who you may be,
a reflection of empty
a heart as cold as ice
chance the dice,
stronger then lies
that I could see,
all
I let myself
foolishly believe,
it was the funniest thing
I just knew
I couldn't trust you
I called you to be
Told you what you needed to see
And like a child
You ran from the truth
I spoke in harsh reality
you feared me
For I am the maiden
And the dragon
I never needed you

A wrong turn

the will to go on

Trusting the ill of heart

a cold grow in my chest

and you know the rest

that shifty look in your eyes,

Suspicion grew

A bad start

tried to move on,

Alone

I have found,

There is no forgiving after love,

Burn me once shame on me

Burn me twice we'll just wait and see

Burn me thrice well that's so unfair

Burn me four times

I'll set your fucking world on fire

laughing at your mere memory

<u>**Heartland**</u>

You are holding in your hand,

Splintered pieces of my heartland

wanting to stay,

echoing pain will remain,

you leave this way

cut to the vein,

never letting the trauma go

It haunted me so,

I always wanted to fly,

fumble and fall apart

a child of a broken heart,

I wanted to be a part of the sky,

wanted love to shine

Inside my eyes,

Enchant the fire inside

Then every hope would die,

you walked out the door

the same as all before,

Words once spoken

Mean nothing to me now,

Everything became a lie

My heart you did defy,

I waited for you

As you asked me too,

Even when I wanted to run and hide,

stayed by your side

there you stand

a crippled

Damaged Man,

Holding in the palm of your hand,

The broken pieces of my
heartland

will I ever trust again?

The town is cold

hallow

and dead,

Love can no longer spread,

We are all covered

In snow and ice,

The harshest winter
of our lives.

Do you ever feel ashamed?
throwing it all away
never had the guts to say,
you wanted things another way,

yes, I agree
it's easier to walk away
than express yourself
fix the problem
I confront these things
for they fester
and I know
you can do so much better

people aren't disposable

False Dreams

Twisted shadows,

learning to let go

He creeps through the seams,

I let love destroy me

every time it would flee,

All I ever wanted was someone

to show me that they care,

I wasn't alone there

left behind

sorrow is never kind,

I can't get you off my mind,

I always hoped that your love was true

love became so evil

So blasphemous,

it started full of happiness

he knew all the words to say,

led astray,

what could he expect of me

you've laid a trap,

full of crap,

did you think

I wouldn't notice

Everything you ever said was a lie,

I have been tricked

I shouldn't go to such extremes,

his heart, a dead machine

Squeezing tighter

as my soul screams,

he killed me with false dreams.

Sometimes lovers

are dressed as lessons

they play that part so well

at the beginning

it's so hard to tell

<u>It's a pain we all know</u>

too well

stabbing in your heart

dreams washed down the well,

we've escaped a hell

we've called a home

twisted shadows follow down,

creeping   to the underground,

Stories filled their heart with selfishness

and

They called it love,

But it burned like drugs

lost, tortured

by a dream.

<u>**Sometimes it's hard,**</u>

holding the demon at bay,

I have only myself to blame,

Every love story ends the same
With a promise and a kiss

Promises too hard to keep,

broken things make us weep

didn't know this hill was quite so steep,

didn't know how to take that leap,

Every love story ends the same,

I only have myself to blame,

with words once spoken,

I tell you of my devotion,

How you caught my soul on fire,

thoughts you inspire,

How we found love,

when we once thought it hopeless

<u>**people are so unkind**</u>

the tragedy they create,

the suffering,   the hate,

In some way, I will make myself see

that love is what makes me,

the suffering I endured

blossoming beautifully blue

With light I assured,

never knowing the meaning

to be loved in return

fighting for myself

open eyes to be

I'll take whatever you throw at me

Because I yearn for better

Nothing hits harder than life

<u>**searched for love in everyone**</u>

devoted my heart completely

to every hand I've touched

stricken to see,

none of them truly loved me,

I have always felt incomplete,

Like

one far off day

true love I would meet,

Always tripping over my feet

Lost in the skies,

dreams reflected in a soft horizon

no matter, the time or season

Love has led me astray,

I become consumed

thoughts in disarray,

always inviting the pain,

Because it always would remain

It's all I have left of all of you

Painful memories

How I learned that lesson

Not everyone deserves the best of me

Look

I've lost control,
trapped in a dark hole,
six feet in the ground
always being down,
I am still looking,
with my wandering eyes,
for the one,
who understands these lines
The one
who never utters goodbyes,
years I have been searching,
for someone kind and nurturing,
a millennium yearning to breathe his atmosphere
for that someone
to heal the hurting
All I have ever done
I've done in the service
of love
it's all I write of,
my heart has a will,
No one can fulfill,
I am always looking still,
Running over the same old ground,
the same thing I found,
for years and years
It's echo ringing in my ears,
Haunting me
with dread,
looking with my wandering eyes,
For the one
who speaks no lies,
nobler than other guys,
he is always wise
With his words
at least he tries
always reach a compromise,
willing to fix things and apologize
Fill our hearts with surprise,
I have been looking, to be swept away,
I have been looking
For a lover who will stay.

Always looking for love
        from the worst kinds of people

        falling in love with their potential

        through the hurting

                I learned to be a healer

Wonder-lust

<u>**you're so wondrous to me,**</u>

I thought it was meant to be,

I'll wait forever,

give you your time

Whatever you need I'll provide

just to be by your side

you're everything I've come to dream

Take down your guard

Find your freedom

in my arms

<u>**all this time**</u>

    it's been an adventure

    to the Place Where I Belong,

For the power to stay strong,

        It's a skill I am working on

All this time I have been observing

        What is both loving and

            disturbing

    the sound of birds singing

chirping, my lady lullaby

        Echo these walls

Contemplating conundrum sings

It's these things I'll never understand

    the Love

      the Hate, that seeds

        between all earthlings,

         how could this be

            we claim to care for things

              as we throw
           them away

      I wasn't born that way

       I'll care for you

      Long after you're out of sight

<u>**Lately, I have been crashing hard,**</u>

I've been counting scars,

wishing to be far away

a place where love would stay,

feelings wouldn't change and fray,

I would have a reason

to live another day,

Crash my heart into embers,

So lost no one remembers,

help me

forget the meaning of this life

outstretched beneath the starry sky,

I will once again catch fire,

Burn ever brighter,

No one else could inspire

mysterious desire,

Inferno Septembers

Crush my heart into embers,

with the unforgettable truth,

We are, who we are

somethings we can never change,

we deserve to move on

all the same

<u>Looking through the glass</u>

Leaving you in the past,

Far away

we are,

As empty as dreams,

Looking for love,

to just be,

Looking for divinity

Mirror eyes crystalize

Down the portal hole

Before the past

Beyond the glass

I found a home inside my soul

I had the power all along

Don't mind me

I'm just poetry

A living nightmare

A daily scare

none did

care

you were the only one there,

as you look at me

in that way,

That makes my soul sway,

I hear you say,

"We are all just living a dream,

Nothing is what it may seem,

I'll be on your team,

make the fans scream,

Because you deserve everything,"

And just like that,

You have me trapped,

How could you believe in me?

Have faith in what I can't see,

Love me,

So perfectly,

That I start to see,

A different side of me,

Happy crazy and free,

How I've long to be,

I let this life captivate me,

And I didn't know who to be,

Or how to set my soul free,

I have to believe in me,

I am meant

For so much more,

Then to feel sore,

    I needed a reason,

        To believe in me,

            Remember,

                Who I want to be,

        I deserve eternity,

            Everlasting,

            In the sky,

And even when I die,

    You shall remember me,

        For I am poetry

<u>**Life is a never-ending circle,**</u>

The soil isn't always fertile,

People can be so hurtful,

That is why I entrust my heart to

My dear journal

I never allowed the hurt

to dull my sparkle

even lost in life's maze

always stuck in a daze

Sad because no one stays

No one stopped to understand,

Writing it all down

Letting it all go

It has its own magic

Ya know

<u>**Take me over**</u>

I surrender,

Touch me,

Soft and tender

soul defender,

You were made for me

A God of divinity

Love me endlessly

Sing my soul's symphony

I'd rip out my heart

I'd tear the world apart

To bring you back to me safely,

All pain melts away

When you look at me,

I remember

Our last December,

Your eyes of golden ember

The soft touch of your gingerly skin

The sweet sound of your voice

Calling me your darling,

your everything

Take me over I surrender,

I render my heart,

Unto you

And when

      the radio would sing

              I could see everything,

And when   the angels would dance,

              I gave love another chance,

And when   the light ran thin,

           I would cave and give in,

When   I forgot everything,

             I'd still remembered to sing,

When I lost my wings,

    Melody's love pulled at my heartstrings,

When   others brushed me aside,

    You were the one I could confide,

      my hurt inside

And when   I've felt lost,

You   remind me of the ultimate cost,

And when   my heart started singing a new song,

          You would be humming along,

And when   we've gone everywhere, we can go,

        Our love will still shine and glow

    this I know for You are gold,

Because when everything seems dark,

    You light up my heart.

I'd give you my love to borrow

If you promise

Not to throw it away,

If you promise

Not to let it decay,

I'd give you my heart to fallow

If you promise

Not to just leave,

For my heart will endlessly grieve,

I'd give you my life

my sorrow,

If you promise to always try,

If you promise to hold me

as the world falls,

that's depression sometimes

I'd give you my endless fantasy,

If you never forget today,

If you never forget to say

"I will love you endlessly,

You're my destiny."

<u>**she is the light**</u>

on lonesome dark nights
Angels sing,

a sweet melody

like heaven is touching me

The mirror of silver stone

Shined a beacon of light

Casting shadows aside

It felt like holey healing

burning into my flesh

a goddess among monsters

That face

Glimmering

Glowing

eyes of the moon

staring back at me

she is the light

I've always needed

Life, death my big adventure,

I must be brave,

Courageous,

Call on my joyous light,

I don't need to live in the night,

 take flight,

 light up the sky,

I will not be just a passerby,

I was made to soar,

Even if my heart is a bit sore,

I can see all the beauty,

That surrounds me,

And how even the streets,

Seam to sing,

I can see the life in everything,

Even when I feel dead inside,

Beauty resounds in the depths of my mind,

I will fly in the sky,

After all,

It hurts to survive

<u>**Longing**</u>

for another

midnight song lover

not any old-soul would do,

got my sights set on you

a fever a passion, in his eyes

A devotion that shines

bright as any star,

To be loved for who you are

The bliss I feel

when he is kissing me

An oh so selfishly

I want him for myself

But captive birds

won't sing the same

I couldn't cage

Such a wild being

I want him to be free

And still choose

to come back to me

<u>**years pass**</u>

as they will,

yet they seem still.

Things change

remaining the same

why are we still playing this game?

strive a will to survive

giving into faith

staying here till we get it right,

are we young or are we of old soul?

love to be bold

our minds explode

on someone unknown,

if only they were open to see,

Everything flows within us

In spirit kind

We who believe

Are the weavers of beautiful reality

<u>**No matter what they say**</u>

I believe the voices calling
     someone out there,
         Something more than this,
            Someone as Haunted as I
     forever taunted
Dreaming
   somewhere out there
        someone to care,
  Lost in thoughts
   and holy rhyme,
     Always needing alone time,

   What can I do,
always needing you,
     I long to be whole
Find the one
    who dances with my soul,
  I want the dreams I see,
To feel you inside of me

<u>Dare this drifty dream</u>

Wonder a bondless thunder

Here and the ever after,

this memory

this daring dream

over skies of gold

Oh, that makes me wonder

what a wondrous wonder

Dreams only make it so far

the here and the ever after,

Memories remain

it is not all the same,

Hearts and Thunder

Faster into this Worldly Disaster

you are my here and the ever after,

Before a time of you and me,

we were meant to be

It was written in the stars you see,

there is no stopping me

I could tell you of this master

this disaster, that has become we,

Upon a story,

upon a dream,

what could this all mean

my story that I have seen,

Living life for a dream,

Not knowing why,

the sky cries

                    before my damaged eyes

                                        everything looks
                                        like lies,

        Dreaming a bondless plunder,

                Sucking the heart,

                    out of everything,

                    Dreaming upon Storming Thunder,
        Reaching for something more   beyond Wonder
                flying over the world,
        Love me
                if you dare,
                    Say words
                            make me believe you care
                in the end, nobody's there,
        Wondering a bondless plunder
                    Daring upon
                    a Drifty Dream,
                        Love is ever to be,
                            The sorrow is meant for
                            me

                                in the end

                            Inviting death

                    I will it so
        All my questions   have no answers,
                        I am fine on my own,

                I am the only love I have ever known.

<u>**a lovely daydream**</u>

My journey invited me
to cross the planes of time
for you
for love
Darling will be mine
till the blue drips from the sky

Little red box full of rhyme
memories carded in time
"Always forever,
till the end of life
I'll love you beyond a weathering storm"

Your Kisses
are poisonous,
I lost my head
Couldn't remember where I've been
looking down hallways
with no doors
Was it me I was searching for
Wanting love
nothing more.

something in the air

        Blowing me along,

        Humming my midnight song

    the luminance of her light

        screamed with comet clouds

        swirls of color

        beyond a dream

she reached for me

        kissed my face

        whispered to me

          "you were never a waste"

Something long broken healed that night

<u>**There is a power inside**</u>

one could hold

your worth more than money or gold.

you're not a soul to be sold

you were written in stars

sufferers say

let's make diamonds out of you'

and admire your shine

Darkness,

Light,

as there is day, there is night,

balance thought the universe

inside of you and me

we see

why we love so intently

to suffer so contently

we hold this power

to love beyond definition

to suffer before confliction

making it our mission

to heal a shattered world

one heart

at a time

<u>Who to be</u>

never known who to be

a violence that has plagued me

{ *Why do I feel the need to be somebody}*

Wild

whispering to trees

the true nature of me

You say I am not enough

not built tough,

tell me who to be

things I'll never believe

you couldn't force-feed me

I am fierce and free,

Being of creativity,

Life is not a joke,

I feel the words you once spoke,

I fight back the tears,

thinking of those years,

how I became who I am

through sadness the pain,

my teenage nightmare,

a broken horror dream,

locked in captivity.

I am not this wounded creature

Or the horror that was done to me

And I refuse to let those years define me

<u>dreams we had</u>

Conquering the sad,

the love we share

changing the way,

we take care,

Hope we spread,

we would mend

the tragedies we did tend,

Like we

there is no other

settling storms

we rage on

in chaos, nature did create

fire faery fate

to dote love,

over-shadowing the hate

<u>**Do you know**</u>

what you do to me
how long
this love wished to be
you could see,
I've longed to be free,
From this demon inside of me,
How to tame the beast,
to conjure a smile,
I have not felt like this in a while,

the deep look in your eyes,
I'd give you everything that's mine,
I would fight against time,
I would crawl on hot coal
I'd give you my soul,

my darling
My endless dream,
My everything,

'
show you in every way,
do the best I can
a simple way to say
I'm always there
I care

<u>Dancing Heart</u>

Sing to me
she tried too much

my very soul could

quiver

SHAKE

Swimming in feelings I crave to make,

to feel my heart dancing

Fierce and free,

how a Faery should be,

All of the love I hold inside of me,

breaking through

looking for something new

Something I can hold on to

All my heart's desire

is you

with all that you do,

my heart dances

soul quiver and sing

what love is supposed to mean

<u>Healing</u>

long

forgotten impressions

my heart's everlasting desire

I burn and turn

ash into the fire,

letting go

what no longer flows

Consuming madness,

The great storyteller

There is nothing in this life I wouldn't do,

to experience love

to be embraced

To keep them safe

Even if

they seldomly see me

can't believe me

inevitably I fight for love,

eternally rise above,

Unto the clock stops

I defend my mermaid heart

<u>**That girl**</u>

She tastes like adventure

And smells of the rain

Her hair was as wild

As a shriek howling bane

Her spirit as constant

as mid-summers wind

With eyes that shined

of emerald green

Her touch

Felt like fire to me

It burned a whole

inside my soul

Only she could fill

<u>**Phoenix rising**</u>

burning ash

over a broken home

I rise

from the ashes and soot

reignite

a flame of the night

taking flight

You can't knock me down,

I will be

flying in the sky

while you're stuck on the ground.

<u>**I get lost in myself**</u>

when I think of back when,

how we overcame

time and time again,

No matter how many tears I cry,

I will not allow it to make me sad inside,

just remembering the good times,

we had a Happy home

a special place we called our Own,

Everything Changed

when we lost our Dad,

These memories

used to make you mad

thinking of what we could've had,

Realities always change,
In our hearts
we remain so much the same,
Even though

our family broke apart,

We still carry them in our heart

all wounds heal in time

I feel better when I rhyme

when I Dance

and Sing

in a forest of ember green

Remembering

the beauty in everything,

There is magic in song

Entranced by a dance

Forgotten fly along

Stars enchant the last chance

to love beyond the hurt

to heal a wounded heart

to honor the magic

in everything

<u>**These Violet days**</u>

Run through violent hours

broken heart sours

killing all that flowers

a feeling overpowers

With a kiss

they do consume,

To tell a story

give a lie

In the end, we all die

make the most of each day

hoping the feeling won't fray

giving birth to decay,

streaming agony, from dismay,

Running through

violent hours,

Opening thousands of doors,

Searching for a way,

A place to stay,

She seems to hide

the key in mind,

only apply

if you keep forever in mind

<u>**He has Working man hands**</u>

sawdust and seas

he smells like apple pie

it's a shouting sign,

when tender words

He couldn't comprehend

nothing goes to plan,

I need to know how to stand

His presence beckoned me,

Took my hand

the romantic in me

egger and adventurous to follow

My lord unto the end of the world.

With a flash, our reality swirled,

Is such a fragile love

destined to outlast time

will I always want what was never mine?

<u>**Damage**</u>

Inside of me

    is all I see,

        How such sorrow

            created me,

    At times I was bitter

          I didn't know any better,

            I faced an endless winter,

     At times I was cold

          My story was yet to unfold,

   I've been a fool

       been a friend,

    I've saved a life

       been lost in death,

   I've set myself free

     Just too yet again

        capture me,

I have lost

    I have learned,

      felt like giving up,

           like

              I just was not enough,

Yet,

    with all I let myself believe

          I came to shine

            with this darkness of mine,

all this Damage that came to be

    for it's the very thing that makes me,

for as long as I can remember

I've wanted to be free

from the shadow

inside of me,

I never stopped to think,

I am so much more

than endless sorrow,

I am far from being hallow,

There is so much life

Flowing through me,

So much

I still dream to be,

I know

I can't tuck away my sorrow

Leaving it to an endless tomorrow,

it walks with me

where ever I may roam,

I have a Damaged soul

inside a heart

of silver and gold

I know I shine

For I love larger than life

Stronger than time,

For all that is Damaged,

Is mine.

About the Dark Poet

Crystal Wells is a Poetess, a single mother, trauma survivor. Mental and physical health are very important to her. With a love of the dark and beautiful she is a moon obsessed, faery blessed, night owl, a rock collecting tree-hugging animal activist. You would often find her at home cuddled up next to her seven cats, and two dogs with a book in her hand and a cup of tea at her side blasting rock n roll. She has been writing poetry since she was twelve years old. Poetry has always been her healthy outlet for all her feelings. It took great courage to share these things.

So, if you wanna go for a ride, to the unfamiliar sound, of the lost being found, get in the car with her.

Let her sing to you her sorrow.